In Memory of Tony De Vit

Tony De Vit was far more than the greatest DJ in history. He was the greatest, most respected, pioneering, gifted, loving man, the world has ever had the pleasure of been blessed with. There will never be another.

The first time I met Tony I mediately felt that I found someone I could trust. Someone who would listen. Someone who would work, play, and help me grow, musically and as a person.

My fondest memory was when with Andy we went to Gatecrasher Sheffield. I think it was the second time to gig at this venue residency. Tony ushered me over to the podium saying, “Do what you do.” Which, incidentally, is the name of one of his hit charts tracks.

I will always remember Tony the way I saw him a DJ, a friend, and the father I never had. Love, love, watching down on us from Heaven above Tony De Vit.

Dedicated too

Us the purest people, who did, do, and continue to show nothing but love. You know who you are.

Author's Biography

The author James Cambell Beswick was born on 11th November 1978 in Cheltenham, Gloucestershire. He and his mother soon moved to Sutton Coldfield, West Midlands.

At the age of eleven diagnosed with dyslexia meaning there was a difficulty with reading and writing. As a result, a move from everyday schooling to a private school that specialised in helping dyslexics.

After one year there was a move back into mainstream education. In an additional same period off to a boarding school which could also support his study difficulties. When seventeen diagnosed with mental health.

Index

Introduction

This account is about how James destroyed almost everything because of his despair and loneliness. At the end of his greedy, power for filled, murderous, lustful life. When the only things that remained were him, and the final source that protects existence saying, “Change yourself and I’ll let you have peace,” finally he did the right thing.

Where it Began

Before the Universe existed, there was just Heaven. Every God lived within this holy plain. Lucifer fell in love with one of the Goddesses. This was classed immoral. He was cast out. Creating anti-matter and matter.

This Devil then had a spell cast upon him. Making him half animal and half man. Anti-matter – alpha male (alpha male meaning a head male animal) the Devil's prison and matter – male the God's new dwelling.

In desperation not standing for this and yearning for his love. Coming back fighting. The two worlds collided. Thus, the Universe was created. Earth was positioned as the centre of entirety. This cast out Demand-God was imprisoned within.

Adam and Eve were then created in the image of the Universes Creators. These first two known beings were teachers. Assigned to be followed by a world of soles in the hope that this demand would one day learn from his mistake. He did not.

Sent as a further test a serpent came lulling the two leaders to eat from the Tree of Knowledge proving there was no alteration to his devilish ways. After doing so the life forms were given the earthly form humans still have today. On the premise that this would make a difference.

PTO

Years went by and the Devils' behaviour did not alter. In response a huge meteor was propelled that struck earth. Which in turn nearly distorted all life completely. This created three furthering tests, countries, races, and religions. Nothing changed and soon further trials to show possible purification were emplaced.

Lust, greed, and control. Time pasted and still there was no sign of him changing. Jesus was then sent to die for our sins in hope that this would make him pure once again. Forget ably there was no change.

New Days Ahead

“Bye Mum, bye Dad.” Julie said kissing her parent’s goodbye, on her way to train as a nurse, at the main London Hospital, Wynn Church. The year was 1967. Being 18 and having a long drive ahead from Moor Oaks, Birmingham to the destination she set off.

Arriving at the hospital, parking, taking her bags out of the car. Julie headed for reception and was greeted by the receptionist, who gave directions to lodgings. Whilst heading over a bag handle snapped and belongings went everywhere.

A handsome man named Albert who was training to be a General Practitioner came over to help. The two instantly began chatting as they both walked over to where the accommodation was situated. They could not take their eyes of one another. Smiling, laughing, and flirting with each other. It was love at first sight.

By 1974 the two were married and went to live in Swindon at the Prince Manton Hospital. 1977 came and both were now living in Cirencester where the two finished training.

Soon, they were living with his parents in Cheltenham. Everything from the outside appeared to be fine. Husband was working as a GP and wife as a nurse at the same practice.

An unorthodox relationship began. After admitting the affair to partner she left. The relationship was now over. Expectedly, three months prior to leaving Cheltenham a son was born, James.

Catastrophically, for the boy the spilt between the now ex-couple leaving him to be brought up by a family that showed no care, no remorse, and no love to James, let alone to one another. James' future seemed bleak.

In his Mothers innocence she decided both move back to Birmingham. To live with her parents Sir Hobert Dolls-Worth CBE and Lady Camilla Dolls-Worth. In time, mother and son moved to a house of their own.

Nearing the boy's third birthday he joined Nelson Hill Nursery School and met his first friend Neva. James used to take much pride in making his new favourite companion laugh.

One term given the lead role in Noah's Ark. During the publicised dress rehearsal. Instead of singing, "Come by ah my Lord," he sang, "Come by car my Lord." As he prodded Neva with a large fig leaf.

In another term, James was chosen to be part of the maypole dancing team. On the day of the dance with parents, teachers, and pupils watching. Making his own run. The pole bend to one side. After time, the two companions lost contact with each other.

When James was five, he moved to Cotton Junior and Middle School. Here he met Hadden. Under his Mothers influence they became best friends. Their interests were the same and they seemed inseparable. Building Star Wars dens, having sleep overs, and watching movies.

During a lunch break at the school James whilst digging in the playing grounds woods. Came across what appeared to be a green gem. After much passing around, the supposed stone-gem was taken by the staff on duty. Years late, the now official jewel that declares the owner by spiritual right the King of England was stolen from the Crown Jewels.

James whilst attending this school went to Nanny Eden's where he underwent years of abuse of every kind. When he was twelve, he started at a day school which specialised in dyslexia. Whilst here he struggled a little but still studied hard keeping up with his subjects.

He studied so well that James was told he would be put up a year and could achieve ten GCSEs with top marks. That he would also, pass A Levels and go on to complete a degree. Unknown to the rest of the pupils the Headmaster did something to James that left him completely brainwashed.

As well at this point in his life James began inhaling propane gas with his cousin. She told him, “It will be a break from reality.” James tried it. He was hooked. Almost instantaneously his behaviour took a turn for the worst.

There was a pupil that used to annoy James. Sometimes for the whole of brake, this pupil would line up first in the queue before returning to lessons. Before entering the school, he would block the only entrance.

The pupil would stop and place his bag in the middle of the doorway. Then he would pull out the essentials for the up-and-coming couple of classes. Taking five minutes or so because what was required was right at the bottom of his bag.

Whilst he was doing this, he would stick his bottom in the air. The boy would then put his bag back and casually stroll on. Even James’s classmates were getting sick of him because the boys’ behaviour would get the whole class detention. They had repeatedly told him to sort his bag out prior to the remaining day ahead. James thought he would teach the boy a lesson.

One day James lined up behind him. As the class were told to go into school, the boy began the usual palaver. Pulling out of his pocket James produced a safety pin which he had stolen from his Mum's sewing basket. He prodded the boys' right butt cheek. The boy flew in the air. Rolling around the floor in the corridor. Yelling his head off. His bag and books were now everywhere. "No detention today everyone." James proudly told his classmates.

On another occasion when school had finished, some of the pupils would often be driven to the station by the Headmaster in the schools' minibus. Which on most days would be driven down a one-way street the wrong way, reason being was that the Master would be trying to get the pupils on the express train home.

Having arrived at the station they would sometimes then jump onto the train whilst it was beginning to move away. Back in those days you could open the train doors even if trains were moving and the windows would open right down.

Once on the train. They used to soak toilet roll under the cold-water tap. Sometimes there would be six to eight of them lined up each by a window of a carriage. On approaching Brewers Lane Station, they would get ready.

One boy would then lean out of the window and shout, "Fire!" Everyone would then throw wet toilet roll at the train guard because when a train went express through a station a guard used to stand on the platform and blow his whistle.

On one occasion the guard was hit right in the face. Preventing the whistle from sounding. The train stopped. Reversing back. They sat down. Pretending that they did not know each other. Which was quite difficult as they were wearing the same school uniform. They were told off and the lad that had shouted got a five-pound fine, which in those days was a lot of money.

Before long James moved back into mainstream education. At this school James was hardly ever there. Being absent from school meant his grades suffered and so did his behaviour. He decided to join a gang, 'The May Way Gang.' This is where James' behaviour deteriorated further.

Loitering is Now a Crime

On his first visit to meet the gang, James turned up with his friend Hadden. Whom he met at Cotton School. Members of the gang kept encouraging James to have fights with them. Luckily, a quickly made friend Eston who in time became incredibly good friends with James stopped the potential forthcoming incidences.

James then joined the Youth Club where most of the gang members hung out. After the Club had finished, they would go and sit in the May Way bus stop.

Unluckily, James now progressing with his drugs taking two bottles of Tippex thinner a day, smoking cannabis nearly every weekend, LSD (Acid) when it was available and poppers the illegally way, things were getting worse.

Whilst hanging around the streets with youths of ranging ages, there were some fun times. On one occasion during rush hour traffic James and some of his friends pretended to be two different groups. Some on bikes and some on foot. Whilst crossing over a Zebra Crossing from both directions. Colliding into each other. Falling over on the road in the centre of the crossing. Motorists would sound their horns and shout at them.

On other occasions members use to go down to the local Chinese Takeaway Restaurant shouting abuse at the staff. Which in turn would result in them been chased down the road with knives.

One night about twenty of the gang went into the local park till the early hours of morning. Taking Acid. During that night they came across what they believed was a pond.

There was no way around it. Except to go back the way they came or walk through it. Some decided to go back. The rest of them had the time of their lives. One member was thrown into the pond. "It's frozen over, hang on," the lad acknowledging that it was not a frozen pond but a grass field.

Later that night whilst looping back to find the others. Someone shouted, "Look it's the Klu Klux Klan!" Quickly everyone picked up logs and stones to defend themselves.

"Get ready. We'll take them on. We'll have um. Ah man, they're even in robes."

"Hey it's us." The group then realised that it was not who they believed it to be, but it was their friends.

One-time the word was spread that there was a party taking place. Spreading across three acres of carparks. James was sick and tired of been called a stupid rich kid. So, he told his friends, "Tell the surrounding areas that the Lord Majors Grandson is having an eighth birthday party here in May Way. With marquees, free food, and free alcohol, and guess what, free drugs. As much as you want, all that you want."

A couple of weeks later hundreds of youths turned up to gate crash. Finding there was no party. The gate crashers got angry. Setting out to look for James they were going to beat him up.

These boys were nearly full-grown adults. One boy walked up to James asking him, "Are you James Trueman?" James took one look at him, the lads behind and said, "No he's over there in the bus stop." The boys walked over. James walked off quickly. Running as soon as he was out of sight.

In the end the whole of the May Way Police Department had to shut the party down. Even Police Officers that were off duty had to attend.

Due to this sort of behaviour James was asked to leave this school too. He was then sent away to a military, multicultural, private, boarding school. Which was another school that specialised in helping dyslexics.

In his first year James was very badly bullied so during this year he became extremely interested in exercise. Which fortunately, meant that there was hardly any need in his eyes for drugs.

James soon became a fourth-year pupil and was now back using and had found a new way to feed his habit, plus make some money at the same time. He became the school drug dealer. When progressing to fifth year he was bringing in two ounces of cannabis a week. James even had the Deputy Head and the Head Boy involved.

When returning to school to avoid getting caught James would hide the cannabis in his girlfriends' handbag. Then when the teachers had searched through his belongings. James's girlfriend would then pass the drugs to him via his bedroom window.

One day whilst at this school James and an associate friend were in the school woods smoking when James's friend said, "I want to go back to your house every weekend and I will handle everything. You can tell your friend's that they can go to hell." At that moment, the Head Boy walked up behind him. Grabbed James's friend and told him, "Leave things well alone."

Incidentally, James would never give any cannabis to any of the girls. Nor to the first, second and third-year boys. When moving up to the fifth year, he never sold to the fourth year. He could not trust these pupils.

Whilst at this school one evening James and his classmates dared a boy to climb on top of the school swimming pool bubble. It was eighteen feet high and kept the pool clean and warm.

As James's friend started to run over the top. His foot became caught and he fell over. Dropping his trainer into the pool he shouted, "I've dropped my trainer."

"I have an idea," James replied, "why don't you drop the other one in then we'll say someone must have put them in there and you couldn't find them after swimming?"

The next day teachers guessed straight away what they had been doing. Persistently, asking James's good friend what he had really done with his trainers as they noticed there was a big hole in the roof.

On another occasion James and his mates made a den. It consisted of three large bits of stolen wood, four or five boxes to sit on. A chunk of wood which was chained to the loft beam. Which in turn made a table so they could roll spliffs.

In the end James was asked to leave this school as well. It was then he hit the Club Scene.

The Endings

For the first part life was bliss. Soon, continued abuse. Mental health issues and his drug use started to become unbearable. Nearing seventeen James had fallen in love with a woman called Sonja and was working on the Club Scene for a man called DJ Symon.

Before long James had lost his love, disappeared from the Scene, and was now living alone. Life for James became even more painful because DJ Symon sadly had died. He had also, progressed into using cocaine daily for some time.

Thinking it was high time to face up to his problems and try to get clean. He decided on going to a drug and alcohol rehabilitation centre. But was kicked out because his behaviour was too unstable. Sometime passed and James was approached by two well-known DJ's.

Both DJ's wanted him to work with them in clubs once more. They came up with an idea for a chart hit. Which was a success. As a now re-establishing DJ, he came up with another idea for a further movement to the exciting one the Revolution. Calling his, the Rebellion. Alongside furthering plans from the three and very quickly his career as **James Trueman the Named DJ**, was successfully redeveloping quickly.

James progressed onto have a radio show and with, chart hit after hit soon he was known as the most popular DJ of all time. He then started another movement the Revolt. James was now undefeatable. Unknowingly to many though, he was becoming more uncontrollably and aggressively mentally unstable.

By 1999 James had built such a career for himself he became a household name. Dew to this, he was signed to do a website gig which was to be shown worldwide. In every bar, club, place of work and residence. On the eve of the millennium James planned he would use this opportunity to start a war for the freedom of drugs.

Thankfully, before it was too late James reached out. He had a visit from two mental health workers. After confessing. At 11pm that night he was sectioned. James spent six years in a mental asylum.

Whilst in hospital, he took a liking to classical music. After being cleared fit to be in society once more. He created his final movement, the Revelation. However, during his period in the institute he not only concentrated on creativity. He pondered evaluating what was really been told to him by staff and the truth about the build up to institutionalisation.

PTO

The Mental Health Workers including top Consultant Psychiatrist Doctors were telling him that he had Bipolar and Schizophrenia. Which in Mental Health Terms is a diagnosis called Schizoaffective Disorder.

James on the other hand knew better. He would not be beaten knowing fully well that, the things that the physicians were saying to him that were not true, James knew they were, and because of this he wondered if there was a deeper meaning to the way he had been living.

The Cold Hard Truth

On the day of discharge James began to think over what the mental health staff were saying to him was untrue. Remembering something that happened to him when he was five years of age. He could remember being alone in the back garden. From nowhere a man appeared. Grey in complexion. Very thin and looked like he was in a lot of physical, mental, and spiritual pain. As James stared in surprise. The man began to speak: James listened and listened well.

The man that James saw before him was his future self. Telling him, “Because of your lack of understanding, empathy, and desire to change yourself. Your selfishness, self-hate and thus, your personal loathing of existence. You are personally responsible for destroying everything as we know it.”

This man went on to tell the five-year-old, “That for the sake of humanity, and the survival of the Universe. All you have to do, is change yourself.” With that the man vanished.

Having had the realisation, that he was personally responsible for killing entirety. He began to work out a way of how to analyse the whole of his past, and hopefully find answer as to him saving not only the world, but all live as we know it.

PTO

James in the same moment realised his true diagnosis and it is ‘too clinically insane to be detained.’

Set in Stone

Laying on his bed at home. James selected a three-hour meditation. He pressed play and began to relax. Concentrating on his breathing. Slowly things began to unravel. His mind moving from differing points.

Suddenly, a significate memory flashed before him, it was of when he sent an e-mail to the rehab he attended.

Dear Simon,

When I was approximately five years old. I used to attend a child minder where I had a good repour in the beginning with everyone.

A boy who was renowned for being kicked out of minders dew to his aggressive strange behaviour. Took a liking to me becoming increasingly more sexually untoward, to the point my life was in danger. I tried on repeated occasions to ask for help. Know, one listened.

At first, I found a moment to open the kitchen knife draw. I was going to react. I wanted to kill. I looked at the knives and said, "Someone or something help me please," as I looked through the window up into the sky above. In that instance I was then shown the consequences and the escape, show nothing but love.

If I had reacted unlovingly, I would have lost contact with Mum, been branded a psychopath, would have been servilely punished, sent to a children's home, (no doubt undergone further abuse) and by now would have probably died of a drug related issue, emotional trauma.

Soon after the woman that was supposed to be the authority figure. Died in her favourite chair of a heart thromboses. Which by the way was where she sat eating sweets, watching TV, and doing crosswords, when I tried for the final time to get help. Having tort, me everything that you did and finding the power of understanding that day it saved my life.

After her death I was finally removed from the minders and even though it has taken me time to get clean. Face up to the emotional aspect of that day. I have never lost site in the acceptance that if I do the right thing I will be protected regardless.

Yours gratefully,

James

Drifting to Fourteen

James' mind then went to a memory, of when he was at his second senior school, where he took an IQ test. Sometime after one of the teachers had a quiet word with him. On marking James' paper, the teacher noticed James had an IQ of a genius.

Later that year over one of the summer school brakes. With his newfound confidence, level of intelligence, and the only hope James had of survival. Due to internal suffering from lack of awareness of himself, and a continuance of forthcoming abuse. Which in turn added to his thus egotistical state. James did something that changed the history of Portugal altogether.

Using an opportunity to communicate with the appropriate authorities. Telling them how to solve a problem that was slowly developing. James in doing this was personally responsible for starting the decriminalization of illegal drugs, and years later solving the countries drug abuse problems. Which in turn also developed a new method of recovery, connection.

Flowing up to Fifteen

Focusing on when hitting the night clubs finding a central night club in Burton. Attending in the beginning on weekends. James' attendance soon became very frequent. His desire to meet DJ Symon became clear. One of his friends and a homosexual man became jealous. They wanted in. James refused.

In response. Under the planning of James's friend. The man pushed his way into a taxi one night and convince James to go back to his house as mates. This was to be the start of a six-mouth abusive sexual conquest to push James into having sex with the man. Which would hopefully end James' journey for fame. Unfortunately, it ended in death yet again.

During this period James on several occasions told the man he was not interested. In the end the man decided to put his old school-tie around James' throat. Telling James, "Sleep with me or I'll kill you." With which James found the strength to throw him over his head and brake free. The man once having regained his confidence. Followed James home and tried to make friends. James declined.

A couple of months later James had a phone call from the man, "I'm really sorry. Let us go out and pull girls." James accepted. On that evening James beat him up and was never bothered by him again.

In reaction to this on returning to the club. Members used James' venerable state of mind to push him into child prostitution. Then one of them decided they should try to convince James to kill himself.

Luckily, James had the gift of servile and all he wanted to do was keep living in the right way. In return, again he showed nothing but love. Knowing fully well that their evil behaviour would result for a second time in his erroneous attitudinal favour.

Drift into Sixteen

Still in meditation James recalled whilst working on the club scene for DJ Symon. His behaviour had become very complacent. He lacked responsibility for his own life, had little insight as to why, in his eyes it appeared that he had the ability to kill with his mind. James had little knowledge as to how living in accordance, with his illnesses and difficulties should be. Resulting he began living promiscuously. Hurting others and mostly himself.

Here something happened to James that even he felt was totally unbelievable. He could recall one night whilst asleep. A bright light came from the other side of his bedroom. Startled James froze in bed. As he did so three men appeared. Accompanied by what seemed to be another him.

The next recollection James had was looking from the other side of the room. Where he first saw the other person that looked just like he did, but only now at himself lying in bed. He could see how thin, rundown, and riddled with disease the old him looked.

The men then explained to James that his importance in the future was of such cruciality, that he must stay alive. With that the men ushered the clone towards them, turned, walked into the light, and were gone.

What had happened prior to that night was that the people with the abilities of time travel and superpowers saw James' death way before he did.

Flow onto Seventeen

At this moment during the meditation James' mind was at a point where he had moved away from home for the first time and was renting a house in Termworth. It was at this place of residence, that his day-to-day usage of cocaine became distressingly worrying even to him. One night whilst he was sitting at home alone, he remembered something that had happened between him and one of his girlfriend's a few years earlier.

On several occasions James somehow could tell his girlfriend was of Irish decent. James then saw a memory of a day when they were at a shopping centre. Near to the entrance there stood a man by a table. With a computer on display. They went over.

The man explained that this computerised facility had a data base installed which could trace family names, giving a brief history of the name and their family crest. Straight away James told the man his girlfriend's surname. The machine brought up information on her past relative's background. There was no crest. But sure, enough though. She was Irish.

James leaving his body present and letting his mind wonder. Then went back to when he was in his rented house in Termworth alone once more. Looking at himself in the mirror. He recalled gazing long and hard. As he did this, he began to establish his bloodlines. More astonishingly he acknowledged his Royal status.

Deeper Still

Floating further James unwound the truth of a day in history which had troubled him and possibly was the one of the main reasons to his being detained under the mental health act.

James looking over prior events pinpointed where for him the problems may have begun. His mind again was at the point back in the shopping moral with his girlfriend. Noticing in his thoughts he placed his family name into the computer as well.

The generation descendant name according to its brief history clearly stated that Cambell, the name was founded in both Scotland and mainland England. Soon after, a war that even the media portrays Scotland and Ireland winning verses England and Wales.

He then recalled reading a document that clearly states the Campbell Clan were the official first rules of the United Kingdom. James then began to surmise why he was not officially King. Concentrating. Slowly but surely, he placed himself as an on looker, to a moment after the battle was won and the documentation had had the Campbell Clan Official Royal Stamp.

On a day following into night. The document vanished. Half of the Campbell Clan fled to the British believing the spirits where against them winning the war. Leaving the now Cambell Clan remaining, they too believed the same.

Then English troops were sent to slater. An English-General who was the most ruthless, loyal solider led. In his ignorance he came up with the name of the Cambell.

The women and children found safety. Opposing sides went to battle. Through continued pure unannounced blind rage, the General was the only man to remain. He then decided to track the remaining bloodline. Beaten. Cover in blood. He collapsed.

The women and children waited and waited. Their men never returned. Then the older women safely hid their children with the younger female generations. Setting off to look for their loved ones. On returning they came across the General. He was barely concussion. The women horrified stood with doubt for the safety of their men. Gazing over at the beaten worrier.

Suddenly, a cloud began to appear between them. A man walked slowly out from the middle. Holding the documentation. It was James. The General jumped to his feet. James then started to explain to them, that the unity between one of the women and the Cambell was crucial to the ongoing survival of existence.

PTO

James also, went on to tell them that he himself was an offspring of both parties. There was total silence from the two sides. One of the youngest women walked forward taking pity on the wounded General. He was never seen again.

In addition, as to what happened yesterday is really another incident that does not need answering. Yesterday is done. What happens today is vastly more important because tomorrow could never come.

Now Eighteen

Arrogantly during the meditation James looked over at the world. Drawing up what he recommended as conclusions.

He noticed unfavourably that in past what the Royals where doing was technically correct but because of the old obsession for power, from all sides. It failed. Going into any relationship with the wrong intentions in his experience usually results in failure. Leaving the next generations innocence to guide the way of love and therefore combine for example the remaining monarchies, bring about World Unity he thought is key.

Winding the Tape Forward

James now using another of the methods he had learnt in the rehab. Began to work out what he had done in his before life. Therefore, what would have happened if he had eventually not told the younger him about the future.

Irresponsibly he would have spent his life obsessed with time-travellers, superhumans and the powers of spirituality. In time, he would have developed an evil belief. Believing that he had movement to and from Heaven. Philosophising that he was the only person to have found the very purpose for the existence of man. Whereas the philosophy for the meaning of all living things is individual.

He then noticed something else that is always equated with individualism. Recalling again whilst in the rehab during his stay at this facility, Simon, and him, developed a sixth conception of reality. Belief. The first is truth, then religion, understanding, faith, and the 5th is spirituality.

Then his mind moved back to what would have become if he had not done the right thing, by telling himself about the future and how to change it.

The Portuguese drug problems would have never had a starting point to been solved. As a result, anger in Europe would have swelled. On the strike of 2000 James would have used the New Year's Eve show as a braking point to start war.

Slowly conflict would have spread to other countries of the world. People rioting believing there was no other way as of a lack of hope in the persons that should be helping them. The four biggest remaining kingdoms Russia, China, India, and Pakistan would have refused to step in. The remaining nations of the world would have agreed.

The reason for these outstanding populations for not reacting, would have been that they knew fully well, with places of population such as the United States of America, the United Kingdom, Australia, and the whole of Europe in terminal, it would have meant utter butchery for their people. In time, rioters would have taken control. Going onto cause total devastation throughout the rest of the planet. Global chaos would have been the result.

The Royal Families, World Leaders and Governments would have abandoned earth. In the outcome that this would hopefully show true unconditional love. Nothing would have changed.

Then the button would have been pressed by those who have little truth of what was coming next. Due to the impact of the nuclear weapons the world would have exploded. The Devil would have been freed. All known existence would have then ceased. Leaving no one other than James and the very source that would have protected him if he had done the right thing.

Change Forever

The meditation music stopped. James opened his eyes and stared up at his bedroom celling. Thinking over what he had seen. He noticed that yes. People had wronged him, and he had wronged others but as he sat now, he was hurting no one and no one was hurting him. Finding acceptance around the mistakes he had made and others towards him.

However, he was still internally not at peace. Closing his eyes again for a moment he could see a bright light shining above him. Concentrating on it and feeling like he was been held aloft. He could see the very power he realised in that moment did and will protect him. This source was not for evil purposes. It was then he noticed his internal pain and suffering had disappeared. He felt whole and content.

James now understood what was needed for him to keep living and in the right way. He had to work a spiritual program and take medication every day. In doing this James would keep his illnesses at bay and his dyslexic difficulties would improve. Resulting, a live being happy, exciting and for filled.

He also realised that in his journey to finding his inner peace, acceptance of reality he had saved not only the World and the Universe but effectively the Heavens too.

PTO

Sometime went by and James became very established, musically, politically, and friendly with the world's dictators.

One day whilst having coffee, comfortably alone. James saw something in the corner of his eye. He turned his head and saw a middle-aged heritage gentleman. James froze realising it was a spirit, "Do not fear," the gent said, "my name is also James, it is time." In a flash of light, the two were stood in a large cave. Looking around, up, and then down. They noticed on the floor encrypted where the words Touch to Repent. James knew what he had to do and why.

Therefore, it was Jesus that died for our sins, but it was James that saved us. Oh yeah, and one more thing, it is a lot harder to do the right thing than it is to do wrong. We are humans and we live on.

The End

www.ingramcontent.com/pod-product-compliance
Ingram Content Group UK Ltd.
Pitfield, Milton Keynes, MK11 3LW, UK
UKHW050613260726
13967UKWH00008B/2840